FICTION PACING

by Rayne Hall

FICTION PACING: PROFESSIONAL TECHNIQUES FOR SLOW AND FAST PACE EFFECTS

by Rayne Hall

Cover design by Erica Syverson and Jasmine Bailey

© 2019 Rayne Hall

November 2019 Edition

ISBN: 9781713271192

All rights reserved. Do not resell, reproduce or distribute this work in whole or in part without Rayne Hall's written permission.

British English

TABLE OF CONTENTS

Chapter 1
WHEN TO SPEED UP AND WHEN TO SLOW THE PACE... 7

Chapter 2
PARAGRAPH LENGTH 10

Chapter 3
SENTENCE LENGTH 12

Chapter 4
WORD LENGTH 16

Chapter 5
DIALOGUE 18

Chapter 6
THOUGHTS, INSIGHTS, CONTEMPLATIONS 20

Chapter 7
EMOTIONS 23

Chapter 8
FLASHBACKS AND MEMORIES 26

Chapter 9
ADJECTIVES, ADVERBS, VERBS AND NOUNS 29

Chapter 10
SIMILES 32

Chapter 11
EUPHONICS 35

Chapter 12
LISTS 38

Chapter 13
DESCRIPTIONS 41

Chapter 14
ACTIVE AND PASSIVE VOICE 44

Chapter 15
PRESENT PARTICIPLE PHRASES 46

Chapter 16
SCENE OPENINGS 49

Chapter 17
ENDING A SCENE 52

Chapter 18
HOW TO VARY THE PACE WITHIN A SCENE 56

Chapter 19
WHAT TO DO IF THE WHOLE NOVEL FEELS RUSHED . . 59

Chapter 20
WHAT TO DO IF YOUR WHOLE NOVEL DRAGS 61

Chapter 21
LEARNING FROM OTHER WRITERS 64

EXCERPT FROM WRITING VIVID EMOTIONS:
CHAPTER 2: VISCERAL RESPONSES 75

INTRODUCTION

In this book, I'll show you professional techniques for speeding up the pace so the readers race through the pages – perfect for action scenes – and for slowing it to grab your readers by the throat with maximum suspense and heart-wrenching situations.

I'll reveal which pacing level is right for which kind of scene and which techniques serve the purpose best, and also how to vary the pace throughout the story and within a scene, as well as how to fix a manuscript where the pace either rushes too fast or drags.

This is a book for advanced writers. The higher your skill level, the more you'll benefit. For example, you need to understand what adjectives and adverbs are before you study their effects on pace, and know how to write dialogue before you begin to modulate dialogue pacing. Inexperienced writers may not yet have the experience to judge when to apply which techniques how strongly, and may focus on technique at the expense of storytelling. The tools I present here are intended to support, not suppress, good storytelling.

I've structured this book as a seminar on fiction pacing – and it can be your guide and companion as well while you're working on your current work in progress (WiP). You can also use it to revise an existing draft where the pacing is off.

We'll start with micro methods – how to optimise the pace for specific sections – because those are easy to master and fix, before progressing to macro issues such as what to do if the whole novel manuscript is a slow-paced drag.

I'm introducing many techniques. I suggest you study them all and absorb the skills, then use your artistic vision to choose the ones you want to apply. Some techniques will feel so 'right' and harmonise with your author voice so naturally that you'll want to incorporate them in all your stories.

As an experienced writer, you may discover that you're using some of the techniques already, either deliberately or by instinct.

If a technique I present doesn't suit your project, leave it out and focus on the others. As long as you understand the how and why of each technique, you can make a conscious creative decision whether to use it.

Many writers use the blue Writer's Craft guides as professional-level training courses in their craft. If you do this, you can set your own curriculum. Study the books not in the order in which I've published them, but mix and match which are most helpful for your current project and your learning ambitions. In some chapters, I'll suggest a Writer's Craft book for deepening your skill in a specific area.

To avoid clunky 'he or she, him or her, his or hers' constructions, I alternate between female and male pronouns. I'm using British English which differs from American English in some word choices, as well as in spellings, grammar and punctuation rules. I hope the Americans among you will appreciate the difference and not assume that unfamiliar spellings are wrong.

This book is short. I could have padded it out to make it longer, but decided to keep my advice to the point and give you the undiluted essence.

Now let's get started. Ready, steady... write!

Rayne Hall

CHAPTER 1
WHEN TO SPEED UP AND WHEN TO SLOW THE PACE

Inexperienced writers often use the same pace throughout the whole book, and the result is a monotonous rhythm that dulls the reader's enjoyment.

A story that's slow-paced throughout drags, and the readers feel bored. A story that races at a relentless pace leaves the reader behind, unable to get emotionally involved.

Vary the pace throughout the story, matching the pace to the content. Some scenes sparkle when you slow the pace, others when you speed it up.

Contrary to what you may have been told, 'fast' isn't always the best choice. Sometimes, a slower pace brings out a scene's suspense and emotional depth.

So, what kind of plot situation calls for what kind of pace? I've compiled a list, so you can see at a glance which situations need what:

FAST PACE

- Physical fight scenes (battles, duels, brawls)
- Chases (on foot, by car, on horseback)
- Races (sports contests, horse racing, car racing)
- Physical escapes (running, climbing, digging)
- Hurry (moving fast to get somewhere on time)

- Any fast physical action that leaves the Point-of-View (PoV) character breathless

SLOW PACE

- Captivity
- Waiting (observing a suspect, hiding until the villain has left)
- Emotionally harrowing experiences
- Ethical dilemmas
- Relationship conflicts
- Any kind of internal conflicts
- Any situation which is low in physical action but rich in suspense, tension, drama, insight or emotion

CHOOSE THE SECTIONS TO WRITE OR REVISE DURING THIS WORKSHOP

I've structured this book like a workshop, so you can write or revise parts of your WiP (work in Progress).

If you have a draft manuscript for a novel or short story that's not as brilliant as it deserves to be, that's perfect to work with. Alternatively, you can write brand new scenes for your next novel, as long as you've already developed a plot outline.

Consider the plot and choose two sections: one that calls for fast pace, and one that demands a slower pace.

They should be partial scenes, each around 300-400 words long.

You will apply the workshop assignments mostly to these two sections. Keep the 'before' versions, so you can compare them with the 'after' results. You'll notice sharp contrasts, not only between the 'before' and 'after', but also between the revised 'slow' and 'fast' manuscript parts.

ASSIGNMENTS

1. Identify a fast-paced section in your WiP. If possible, choose one in which the Point-of-View character moves fast physically – perhaps a sword-fight, a foot race, or the frantic action to save a burning house. If your story has several suitable scenes, pick the one where the action is fastest. Copy-paste about 300-400 words of it into a separate document.

2. Now identify a slow-paced section in your WiP. The PoV may be involved in a relationship conflict and have to make a heart-wrenching choice, or he may desperately want to take urgent action but be forced to stay still. Don't choose a boring part of your novel: slow-paced does not mean dull. Something happens in this section that keeps the reader enthralled – it just isn't fast physical action. Copy-paste about 300-400 words of it into a separate document.

Don't progress until you've selected the two sections you want to work with, because from the next chapter on, you'll learn pacing techniques and apply them right away.

CHAPTER 2

PARAGRAPH LENGTH

Let's start with a quick and easy technique.

The length of paragraphs creates a sense of fast or slow pace. So by simply making the paragraphs shorter or longer, you can create a different effect.

FAST PACE

In a fast-paced section of your story, paragraphs should be short – typically just two or three sentences. When the action gets super-fast, you may have paragraphs consisting of a single sentence – or even just one word.

SLOW PACE

To slow the pace for a section of your writing, combine several sentences in each paragraph. Between four and seven sentences per paragraph works well.

PROFESSIONAL TIP

Vary the paragraph length to keep the page visually interesting. Break the monotony by including a four-sentence paragraph in a fast-paced section, and a two-sentence paragraph in a slow-paced part.

WHAT NOT TO DO

Avoid very long paragraphs of ten or more sentences. Although many 19th-century classics have paragraphs spanning more than a page, texts with frequent paragraph breaks are easier to process for modern readers, both on the printed page and in electronic format.

ASSIGNMENTS

These assignments are super-easy and will take only a few minutes.

1. In your fast-paced section you've chosen to work with, find any paragraph that has more than three sentences, and insert an extra paragraph break to split it up.

2. Also in your fast-paced section, identify the moment when the action is fastest, and create one or several single-sentence paragraphs.

3. In your slow-paced scene, find any paragraphs shorter than three sentences, and consider combining them. For example, a couple of two-sentence paragraphs might make one four-sentence paragraph. (Obviously, do this only if the content of the paragraphs fits together. Use your artistic judgment.)

CHAPTER 3

SENTENCE LENGTH

This technique is easy to master, though you'll need to spend a few minutes applying it.

Short sentences convey a sense of fast pace and breathlessness. Slow sentences create a more sedate mood.

FAST PACE

For a fast-paced section, short sentences work best. How short? This depends on your writing style, how many words you normally use per sentence. If your average sentence length is 35 words, then 25 words per sentence is fast. But if your sentences are around twelve words per sentence, fast-paced sections will call for eight.

How to achieve this:

1. Cut superfluous words. (In good writing, we cut superfluous words anyway – but in fast-paced scenes we need to be extra-stringent about this.)

Here are two examples:

Instead of

She turned to look at John and suddenly realised that he was still watching her. (15 words)

Write:

John was still watching her. (5 words)

Instead of

He started to wonder if he could really trust Bill. (10 words)

Write:

Could he trust Bill? (4 words)

2. When you find a lengthy sentence, restructure it in two separate sentences. Sentences where clauses are connected with words like *and, but, when, while, therefore* are easy to separate.

Here's an example:

Instead of

When the motor in the street below roared again, John snatched up the suitcase and dashed down the stairs. (One sentence of 19 words.)

Write

The motor in the street below roared again. John snatched up the suitcase and dashed down the stairs. (One sentence of 8 words and one of 10.)

Here's another example, this one provided by my friend Douglas Kolacki, a fantasy author. In the first draft of this pirate story, the sentence read:

He waved his double-barrelled revolver, drawn in a hurry from wherever in the folds of his greatcoat he kept it. (20 words)

A faster-paced version of this sentence might go like this:

He whipped a revolver from the folds of his greatcoat. (10 words)

When the action is super-fast, you can emphasise this with truncated (grammatically incomplete) sentences:

He had to cross that river. Had to. Now.

However, this technique is best used sparingly.

SLOW PACE

To reduce the pace, insert extra words – the kind of words which aren't strictly necessary but enrich the reader's experience.

Create longer sentences by combining two or three short ones into a single longer one. But don't overdo this: modern readers dislike convoluted sentences.

Here's an example:

Mary chose her nail varnish. She applied a pink that matched her frock. (Two sentences of 5 and 10 words)

This could become:

Mary chose her nail varnish with care and applied a soft pastel pink that matched her summer frock. (One sentence of 18 words).

PROFESSIONAL TIP

Vary the sentence length. Sprinkle some medium-length sentences in both the fast- and slow-paced sections. This maintains a lively rhythm and helps keep the readers interested.

WHAT NOT TO DO

Don't write a whole page consisting of just super-short sentences. Otherwise the rhythm becomes monotonous, and monotony kills pace, so you would achieve the opposite of what you set out to gain.

Don't use sentences so long and convoluted that the reader needs to stop, re-read and disentangle it.

FURTHER STUDIES

If you want to learn how to tighten your writing by cutting superfluous words, I suggest my book *The Word-Loss Diet*. Many writers who've applied the techniques report that their writing voice has become so much stronger that they're now getting more acceptances from fiction publishers. But be warned: this book is tough, not for the faint of heart. You need to be prepared for a critical examination of your writing style.

ASSIGNMENT

1. Find the longest sentences in your fast-pace section. Choose one of them for editing. Either break it into two or more short sentences, or prune out unneeded words, or both. Optional: repeat this with other sentences.

2. Find the shortest sentences in your slow-pace section. Choose one of them for editing. Either link it to the preceding or following sentence, or add more words (but only words that enrich the content), or do both. Optional: repeat this with other sentences.

CHAPTER 4

WORD LENGTH

We've looked at the length of paragraphs and sentences. Now let's take a look at words.

FAST PACE

In fast-paced sections, it's best to use short words. Aim for words of one or two syllables, with the occasional three-syllable word. Avoid anything longer unless there is no short word to do the job.

Here's an example for fast-paced action requiring fast-paced writing.

Before:

She accelerated the car.

After:

She stepped on the gas pedal.

Both convey the same content, but the second feels faster because it doesn't have the long word 'accelerated' it.

SLOW PACE

In slow-paced scenes, use a mix of word lengths. It's not possible to avoid single-syllable words in the English language, and you shouldn't even try. (Most prepositions, pronouns, and conjunctions have just one syllable, and you need them to form coherent sentences.) But for other words – verbs, nouns, adjectives – you can give preference to those with two or three syllables. Throw in the occasional four- or five-syllabic word. (But don't overdo it, or your writing will read like a bureaucrat's legal or technical document.)

PROFESSIONAL TIP

As the action speeds up in a fast-paced scene, use shorter and shorter words. During the fastest paragraphs, use lots of single-syllable words.

WHAT NOT TO DO

Don't obsess over the syllable count. The meaning of a word is more important than the number of syllables. Don't get rid of a great word just because it's a little too long or too short.

ASSIGNMENTS

1. Read your fast-paced excerpt. Are there any words longer than three syllables? See if you can eliminate them.

   Could any of the three-syllabic words be replaced with a two-syllabic synonym? If it fits, use the short word instead.

2. In your slow-paced excerpt, flag up any single-syllabic noun, adjective or verb. Think of two- or three-syllabic synonyms to replace them. If you like the synonyms, use them.

CHAPTER 5

DIALOGUE

Both fast- and slow-paced sections can have dialogue – but you need to write the dialogue differently.

FAST PACE

In your story's fast-paced section, characters speak in short sentences, short words and short dialogue lines, almost as if they were out of breath while running.

Most dialogue contributions will fit into a single text line. Cut out every unnecessary word and pare the spoken bits to the essentials.

This reflects reality. People who are running a race, fighting with sabres, hurrying to ready the house for the approaching hurricane, simply don't have the breath to spare for long sentences. They're also too focused on what they need to do to talk more than necessary. Aim to convey that sense of breathlessness.

Example:

Imagine two characters running away from a pursuer who wants to kill them.

"Over there. Let's try. "

"Are you sure? There'll be no turning back."

SLOW PACE

In slow-paced sections, the characters speak normally, in complete sentences with correct grammar.

Example

Imagine two characters sitting on the couch drinking tea.

"We may be able to enter the park through the back gate by the gazebo. That's probably the best option, I think we should try."

"Are you absolutely sure you want to do this? Once we've started, it will be too late to change your mind. There will be no turning back."

PROFESSIONAL TIP

If the characters are engaged in rapid physical action, let them speak in sentence fragments and even single words.

Example: "You ready?"

"Wait. Now."

WHAT NOT TO DO

In slow-paced sections, don't give in to the temptation to use long, convoluted sentences. Those don't sound real in dialogue.

ASSIGNMENT

1. Tighten the dialogue in your fast-paced section. Be ruthless, and pare it down drastically.

2. Optional: optimise the dialogue in the slow-paced scene. Let characters speak in mostly complete sentences. (Your dialogue may already be exactly right in the slow-paced section, so you may not want to change it.)

CHAPTER 6

THOUGHTS, INSIGHTS, CONTEMPLATIONS

Your Point-of-View character's thoughts affect the pacing in a big way.

The more she thinks, the more the pace slows. That's fine if you want the pace to be slow – but devastating if you want the pace to be racing.

FAST PACE

You may need to take drastic, ruthless action in your fast-paced sections.

- As far as possible, remove all thoughts. This includes all wonderings, ponderings, considerations and realisations
- If the PoV character's thoughts are essential to the plot, see if you can move them to a slower-paced section
- If thoughts can be neither deleted nor moved, cut them down to as few words as possible. Be ruthless about this
- Don't use tags (he thought, she wondered) at all
- Postpone significant insights to the next slow-paced section. They will work better there

Example

Before:

She realised that there was no way out whatsoever.

After:

There was no way out.

SLOW PACE

- A slow-paced section is a good place for character thoughts.
- Sharing what the character thinks can enrich the section and give it depth
- Write the thoughts in complete, grammatically correct sentences
- Arrange the words so the thought-sentences have a pleasant rhythm.
- You may include words that aren't strictly essential, as long as they elucidate the meaning or improve the rhythm
- You may include thought tags *(she wondered, he realised)* if you feel they help clarity

PROFESSIONAL TIP

The perfect moment for a character's significant insights is in a slow-pace interlude immediately after a fast-pace section.

For example, John has escaped from the evil overlord's dungeon and is running for his life. For this section, you'll use super-fast pacing, with no superfluous thoughts and no insights.

He hides in a disused latrine shaft, waiting for his pursuers to pass him by. While he's in the latrine shaft and they're searching the ground, he's immobile, mustn't make a sound, mustn't move. (This section has slow pace and high tension.) While he's immobile in the latrine shaft, with his heart still racing but his breath slowing, John's brain connects the dots and he realises who betrayed him: his best friend.

By placing this insight in the slow-paced section following the extremely fast-paced section, you make it believable and give it the impact it deserves.

WHAT NOT TO DO

Don't write long, rambling wonderings and ponderings, even in slow-paced scenes. Otherwise the pace won't be just slow, but dragging.

ASSIGNMENTS

1. Strip all thoughts, wonderings, ponderings and insights from your fast-paced section, as far as possible.

2. Tighten any thoughts that need to stay in this section to the bare minimum.

3. In the slow-paced section, revise any character thoughts so their rhythm flows beautifully. (With or without thought tags, as you prefer.)

4. If your slow-paced section doesn't contain any character thoughts, consider inserting one – preferably an insight.

5. What insights must your character gain around here in this part of your story? What questions might she ask herself, what realisations might dawn on her? Consider placing this insight in this slow-paced section.

CHAPTER 7

EMOTIONS

In this chapter, we'll look at how to handle emotions in connection with pacing.

FAST PACE

In fast-paced sections, the characters are too focused on the rapid action to indulge in feelings.

Rich emotions would not only slow the pace, but feel out of place, not quite realistic.

Keep feelings to a narrow range of raw emotions such as fear, desire, fury and hope. These are plausible in fast-paced sections, and can drive the action.

Don't spend many words describing the Point-of-View character's feelings. Keep them brief, and show how they motivate the character's action.

Example:

Fuelled by fear, she raced across the tarmac.

SLOW PACE

Slow-paced sections are your story's wells of emotion. Here the relationships develop, and characters react with feelings. Allow your readers to feel what the PoV character feels. The emotions can be nuanced, deep and rich.

Let your character feel more than one emotion. For example, she may experience suspicion, distrust, jealousy and resentment at the same time, or one after the other.

The emotions can vary in intensity. The embers of jealousy may burn in her heart throughout the scene, but they will flare up when she sees her lover smile at the other woman.

Example:

The sight of them together burned a trail of fire through her chest.

You can show what the other (non-PoV) characters feel by showing their facial expressions and body language. In a slow-paced scene this will work well, because the PoV has time to watch other people.

PROFESSIONAL TIP

In slow-paced scenes, show several different 'shades' of the PoV's main emotion. For example, if her main emotion is fear, you can put her through apprehension, fear and terror.

WHAT NOT TO DO

Don't write a whole slow-paced scene that consists of nothing but thoughts and emotions. Even slow-paced scenes need action, or they drag.

FURTHER STUDY

If you want to learn how to create character (and reader) emotion, my book *Creating Vivid Emotion* will teach you professional techniques.

ASSIGNMENTS

1. Take the fast-paced scene you've chosen to work with. Have you used emotions? If yes, are they the kind of basic, raw emotion that works in a fast-paced scene? Keep those. Are they complex and refined emotions? Then move them to a slow-paced section.

2. Look at the remaining emotions in your fast-paced scene. One or two are enough. Instead of describing the feelings, show how they fuel the character's actions.

3. Visualise your slow-paced section. Try to experience it from the perspective of the PoV character. What does she feel? Make a list of all the emotions. You should come up with at least three. Emotion-rich stories need more.

4. Find a way to convey each of these emotions to the reader, for example through the character's dialogue *("I've had enough!")*, visceral reactions *(Her stomach boiled with anger)* or actions *(She slammed the door.)*

CHAPTER 8

FLASHBACKS AND MEMORIES

You probably know that flashbacks can halt the flow of a story, and therefore try to avoid them. However, some flashbacks are crucial to the plot.

The solution: place them in the right part of your story.

FAST PACE

Don't allow any memories to creep into the fast-paced section, and don't stop the rapid action to insert a flashback.

This can leave you with a problem: what if it's crucial for the reader to know something that happened before? I'll suggest several solutions under 'Professional Tip'.

SLOW PACE

In a slow-paced section, flashbacks and memories can work really well. So if Mary needs to remember her childhood visits to Aunt Agatha's farm, or recall what John told her last year, put it in a slow-paced section of your story.

PROFESSIONAL TIP

Inserting flashbacks and memories in slow-paced sections is relatively easy. But conveying information that the reader needs to know in fast-paced sections needs professional-level skills.

Let's say John uses a bicycle to chase after Mary. This obviously requires a fast-paced writing style without flashbacks. But the reader needs to know how John got hold of a bike.

Your first impulse may be to insert a flashback. *(John thought back to how he had found the bicycle. His neighbour Bill had left his garage door open as always, so John was able to get in and....)* This kills the pace.

Here are five strategies professional authors use. Choose the one that suits your purpose best.

1. Insert it as 'live' action into the story: *John raced to his neighbour's house. He banged on the door, but Bill wasn't at home. Luckily, the garage door stood open. John grabbed the bicycle, leapt into the saddle and pedalled furiously....*

2. Weave the essential information into the action of the fast-pace section, without flashback or info-dump. Often, three to five words are enough to convey what's needed. *(On his neighbour's bike, John raced after Mary.)*

3. At the end of a preceding slow-paced section, show the PoV's intentions. *(John resolved to snatch his neighbour's bicycle.)*

4. Weave the necessary information into a previous slow-paced section. (Mention in passing that the neighbour's garage door stands open with a bicycle inside it.)

5. In a later, slower-paced version, use dialogue to fill the reader in. *("This isn't your bicycle." Mary glared as if she had just caught him red-handed in a theft. John grinned. "It's Bill's. He always leaves his garage door open.")*

ASSIGNMENTS

1. Identify any flashbacks and memories in your fast-pace section. Delete them, or see if you can apply one of the strategies I showed under the Professional Tip heading.

2. If your PoV character needs to remember something, or if you want to flash back to a past event, insert it into the slow-pace section. You'll need to provide a trigger for switching from the current story level to the past, e.g. the arrival of a letter, meeting someone from the past, or a smell that reminds the PoV of her youth.

CHAPTER 9
ADJECTIVES, ADVERBS, VERBS AND NOUNS

The type of words you use affect how 'fast' or 'slow' a section feels to the reader.

(For this chapter, I assume that you have the basic understanding of what verbs, nouns, adjectives, adverbs etc. are. But I promise to keep it simple and not to delve into complex grammar issues.)

FAST PACE

Adjectives generally have a pace-slowing effect. In a fast-paced section, use them sparingly. You don't need to cut them out altogether, but aim to use no more than one adjective per sentence, and avoid strings of adjectives. Where you need an adjective, choose the shortest one that suits the purposes.

For example, instead of *'his age-mottled, desiccated, wrinkled face'* write *'his wrinkled face'*.

Adverbs have an even stronger pace-slowing effect. Try to avoid them altogether in your fast sections. This is best achieved by choosing vivid verbs that require no adverb.

For example, instead of *'he ran quickly'* write *'he sprinted'*. Instead of *'she sank dejectedly into the chair'* write *'she slumped into the chair'*.

Verbs define the pace of a section. For a fast-paced section, write each sentence so that the verb is the most vivid part. Choose a short verb that creates an image in the reader's mind, or better still, a mini-movie. (Or, if it's something other than visual, then a sound or a smell or other experience.)

Example:

She sat on the chair.

That doesn't evoke much of a movie or image. However, if you choose a more vivid verb, the sentence becomes more interesting, and feels faster paced:

She perched on the chair.

She slouched on the chair.

Nouns have a slight pace-slowing effect. You can't avoid them, and you don't need to. Simply choose short nouns (one or two syllables) where possible, and favour nouns that are descriptive enough not to need an adjective.

Examples: Instead of *'a female dog'* write *'a bitch'*, and instead of *'a young cat'* write *'a kitten'*.

SLOW PACE

Adjectives. The pace-slowing effect of adjectives is perfect for slow-paced scenes. You can use several adjectives in each sentence, even one after the other. Use them to enrich the image (or sound, smell, video) in the reader's mind.

Examples:

Before:

The evening sun cast a glow over the land.

After:

The mellow evening sun cast a soft golden glow over the land.

Before:

Autumn leaves crunched under my boots.

After:

Dry, rust-coloured autumn leaves crunched under my heavy boots.

Adverbs – in moderation – are okay in slow-paced sections. However, use them sparingly.

Verbs in a slow-paced section can be short or long, and they don't necessarily have a greater importance than other words. But they should still be well-chosen and evocative.

Nouns are the most important words in slow-paced sections. Use your creativity to choose the best nouns you can find. You can even indulge in the occasional multi-syllabic noun.

PROFESSIONAL TIP

While it's best to avoid adverbs in fast-paced sections, their use in slower parts depends on the genre. For example, Romance novels generally use adverbs in slow-paced sections, while Thrillers use hardly any.

Model your use of adverbs on the recent bestsellers in your genre.

WHAT NOT TO DO

Don't overdo the use of adjectives in slow-paced sections, because they can make your writing feel 'purple prose-ish' and clunky.

ASSIGNMENT

1. Go through your fast-pace section. Replace dull verbs with vivid ones. If a sentence has more than one adjective, consider cutting them. Get rid of adverbs as far as possible.

2. In your slow-paced section, try to include at least one adjective in most sentences.

CHAPTER 10

SIMILES

In an experienced writer's hands, similes – comparing a new experience to something familiar – are a fantastic tool. A single well-chosen simile can serve many purposes: description of what the PoV sees, characterisation of the PoV, deepening PoV, convey PoV's backstory, convey PoV's attitude, world-building, entertainment, and more.

BUT – the simile needs to be in the right place. Here's Rayne Hall's rule of thumb: "Put similes in slow-paced sections only."

You may want to study the works of Raymond Chandler. His novels in the Noir genre (an early version of what we would today call Thriller) are fast-paced and exciting... and the similes he uses are dazzling.

Here are some examples of Chandler similes:

He looked about as inconspicuous as a tarantula on a slice of angel food.

A few locks of dry, white hair clung to his scalp, like wild flowers fighting for life on a bare rock.

The General spoke again, slowly, using his strength as carefully as an out-of-work showgirl uses her last good pair of stockings.

She looked playful and eager, but not quite sure of herself, like a new kitten in a house where they don't care much about kittens.

Grayson put his bony hand out and I shook it. It felt like shaking hands with a towel rack.

Chandler's works are full of similes – he's famous for them. They never feel wrong, they don't jar, and they don't halt the momentum of the story. How does he do it? He places them only in the slower-paced sections of his novels. (Chandler's novels have an overall fast-pace style, but he modulates the pace skilfully by injecting brief slower-paced sections between the hard action scenes.)

FAST PACE

Avoid similes here.

SLOW PACE

Use your creative imagination to come up with similes that suit the story content and your writing style.

PROFESSIONAL TIP

The very best place for a simile is the slow-pace section where the character urgently needs to do or receive something, but is forced into inactivity, and time is running out. What she observes around her in this situation may well bring on memories of something else, and it can convey her frustration.

You can create a simile around the time running out. (Here's an example of how I did this in one of my novels. *Storm Dancer* is a historical fantasy novel. I wrote: *Time seeped away like oil from a leaking jar.* The novel is set in the Bronze Age, and olive oil is stored in pottery jars, so the simile does double duty for world-building. Since this scene features a wildfire approaching and destroying the settlement, the simile also reminds the readers that there's a lot of flammable oil stored nearby.)

WHAT NOT TO DO

Don't use hackneyed, clichéd similes (as dull as ditch water, as white as the driven snow, as black as the night, as proud as a peacock).

Fiction Pacing

ASSIGNMENT

1. Read through your fast-paced section. Does it contain any similes? If yes, they probably stop the momentum. Do you really need them? Consider deleting them. If you're in love with a simile because it's such a creatively crafted gem, see if you can put it in a different (slower-paced) section instead.

2. Insert a simile (or two or three, if it suits your writing style) in the slow-paced section. This is where you can apply your creative artistry. Craft a simile that's original and just right.

CHAPTER 11

EUPHONICS

The way words sound has a subtle yet powerful effect on the human psyche. The effect is strongest when we hear the words, but it also works when reading.

Certain sounds create a sense of high speed and hurry, while others convey comfort and leisure. If you choose words that contain the right sounds, you can intensify the impression of fast or slow pace.

FAST PACE

The sound 'R' makes everything feel faster. Use words containing an R. Words starting with R, or containing a double R have the strongest effect.

In the English language – which has stronger euphonic elements than any other language I know – many words with fast-paced meaning actually contain R or RR, e.g. 'race' and 'hurry'.

Other sounds that help convey fast pace are K, T and P.

Another euphonic technique for fast pace is to choose words with short vowels.

This technique works especially well if combined with another fast-pace technique – that of choosing short words.

Examples:

He took the risk and hurried to the river.

She grabbed the rucksack and raced down the road.

SLOW PACE

To convey a slower pace, use words with long vowels, e.g. OO, OW, EE.

You can refine this by matching the sounds to the content.

The sound 'L' hints at idle lazy leisure, and also at slow sensuous pleasures. (This can be very effective in erotic scenes.)

Example:

Reclining on the lounger, she lifted a languid hand to signal the waiter.

He trailed his tongue along her lower lip.

The sound 'M' suggests comfort and works well in a cosy setting where the character feels at home. (This is perfect for those short moments when you allow your characters to relax before you throw the next big problem at them.)

Example:

He let the fire warm his tired limbs, and savoured his mother's home-cooked meat and mashed potatoes.

The sound 'OO' adds a note of foreboding and doom. (Use this for situations where the character is in a far from comfortable situation, can't escape and sees the danger approach slowly.)

He watched the moon rise in the soot-black sky.

WHAT NOT TO DO

Don't go overboard with euphonics, and don't sacrifice content for sound. Instead, apply euphonics with a light brush, so subtly that your readers aren't aware what you're doing.

PROFESSIONAL TIP

Pay especial attention to euphonics if you plan to release your story as an audiobook or to give author readings.

FURTHER STUDY

If you're interested in this subject, my book *Euphonics for Writers* deals with it in depth, and covers many other sounds and their psychological effects.

ASSIGNMENTS

1. In your fast-pace section, see if you can replace a few words with others containing R. (You may find that you've already done this during the previous assignments, because English is such a euphonic language that the sound of a word often matches its content.)

2. In your slow-pace section, consider if L (sensuality and leisure), M (comfort) or OO (foreboding and doom) suit best. Try to insert that sound – maybe just once, maybe several times. If none of them apply, skip this assignment.

3. In your slow-pace section, consider if you can replace some words with others that have long vowel sounds (oo, ee, ow....)

CHAPTER 12

LISTS

The conventional way of listing items or actions in a sentence is to separate them with commas, except the last one which gets added after an 'and'.

Example:

She applied powder, rouge, eye-liner, mascara and lipstick.

If you ditch this conventional structure, you can create a different effect:

She applied powder, rouge, eye-liner, mascara, lipstick.

(Without the 'and', this suddenly feels rushed. The reader senses that the character is in a hurry to get her make-up on.)

She applied powder and rouge and eyeliner and mascara and lipstick.

(With 'and' between all the words, this feels tedious. The reader senses that the character is fed-up with having to get all this make-up on.)

Let's look at when and how to use this technique.

FAST-PACED SECTION

Leave out the connecting 'and' and simply list the items with commas. Now it appears that the character is doing this in a great hurry. You can list verbs showing all the character's actions, or nouns for all the objects the character handles. You can either use a pronoun (she, she, I) for each action, or just use one pronoun at the beginning.

Examples:

He hacked, slashed, sliced. (This would be for the extremely fast-paced section of a sword-fight scene.)

He hacked, he slashed, he sliced. (This doesn't have the frantic speed, but great dramatic emphasis.)

She ran, she ducked, she leaped.

He shuttered the windows, slammed the door, pushed the bolt in place.

She tossed everything into her suitcase: passport, toothbrush, denims, underwear.

He tried the front door, the back gate, the windows, the cellar hatch.

This type of list is called 'asyndeton'.

SLOW-PACED SECTION

Lists with many 'and' (or many 'or') convey a sense of tedium. They may hint that the character is bored, impatient or fed up. This is a great way to let the reader feel the boredom... without actually boring the reader. Readers can feel immersed in the tedium for one sentence, without actually having to experience it for as long as the character does.

This is called 'polysyndeton'.

Examples:

John glanced at his watch. His wife was still standing by the shoe cabinet, deliberating whether to wear the pink heels, or the classic black stilettos, or the silver sandals, or the Gucci fakes.

Mary yearned to jump on her mare and gallop across the fields, but the governess made her sketch Doric column shapes and embroider a pious sampler and state the uses of atropa belladonna and recite a poem and decline French verbs.

The speaker droned on about the company mission and the founder's values and the company's history and the outlook into the future and the valuable contributions they were all going to make.

WHAT NOT TO DO

Don't overdo this technique! One or perhaps two list-sentences per scene are enough.

PROFESSIONAL TIP

In a thriller or mystery, a list sentence can serve to let readers see a clue without drawing attention to it. At the time, the reader glossed over the mention of knitting yarn and belladonna atropa.... but when a ball of knitting yarn is found at the crime scene, or the pathologist announces that the victim was poisoned with belladonna, these early mentions take on significance.

FURTHER STUDY

My book *Euphonics for Writers* contains chapters about using lists for modulating rhythm and pace.

ASSIGNMENT

1. Is there a sentence in your fast-paced section where actions or items are listed? If yes, try leaving out the final 'and'. How does it read?

2. Do you want to convey boredom, tedium or impatience somewhere in your slow-paced section? (If not in the section you're currently working on, you may choose a different one.) Could you convey this with a list full of 'and' or 'or'?

CHAPTER 13

DESCRIPTIONS

Descriptions slow the pace. Sometimes this effect is desirable, but sometimes it's devastating.

Here are some tips for using the senses to create descriptions that match the pace.

FAST-PACED

In a fast-paced section, keep descriptions short, and use short words, short sentences, short paragraphs. Focus on vivid verbs with few adjectives. (All these we've covered in previous lessons.)

You don't need to describe much. Choose a single telling detail rather than describing the whole thing.

Don't stop the action to insert the description. Rather, weave the description into the action.

Example:

Instead of

Clapboard façades and wooden hovels lined the road.

write

He raced past clapboard façades and wooden hovels.

The sense to use for fast-paced sections is the sense of hearing. Describe sounds and noises, because these don't slow the pace much, yet create a lot of atmosphere.

Instead of:

Well-fed, brown-and-white cattle grazed contently in the flowery meadow.

write

Cowbells clanked.

Instead of

His mother wore shiny black patent shoes with high tapering heels

and

The floor was diagonally tiled with marble.

Write

His mother's heels clacked on the marble tiles.

SLOW-PACED

In a slow-paced section, devote more words to descriptions. As long as the descriptions are interesting, readers will enjoy them.

However, don't dump a big chunk of description at the beginning of the scene. Instead, place small pieces of description here and there throughout the scene.

Use several senses: seeing, hearing, temperature, balance, tasting, touching, pain, smelling etc.. Aim for at least three senses in each slow-paced scene.

The sense of smell works especially well when the PoV character enters a new environment. Devote a whole sentence to the smell (or combination of smells) of the place.

The sense of hearing can be highly effective in a slow-paced scene as well. Use it while the main character is waiting for something.

Examples: Perhaps the villain is about to burn her flesh with his cigarette. The glowing end comes closer and closer.... This is when she hears water gurgle down the drainpipes, or a distant car door slamming. Or perhaps she has just asked her husband, "Do you want a divorce?" While she waits for an answer, the coffee maker hisses and the radiator clanks.

This increases the suspense.

ASSIGNMENTS

1. Take a fast-paced section. Consider the descriptive elements in it. If there are none or not enough, add some. If the ones you have are slowing the pace, replace them. Where it makes sense in the plot, use sounds to describe people, actions and settings. Keep the descriptions short. Where possible, weave the descriptions into character actions, rather than present them as standalone sentences.

2. Take a slow-paced section. Improve the descriptions. Delete excessive descriptions. If you have only or mostly visual descriptions in this section, replace some of them with other senses. If the character enters a new location, describe what the place smells like. If there's a moment when the main character waits for something (an action or an answer) insert one or several background sounds.

CHAPTER 14

ACTIVE AND PASSIVE VOICE

Passive Voice sentence constructions have an extremely pace-slowing effect.

FAST PACE

Be strict: eliminate all Passive Voice from your writing in sections where you want the pace to be fast.

Examples:

Instead of

I was bitten by the dog.

Write:

The dog bit me.

Instead of

The ship was captured by the pirates.

Write:

The pirates captured the ship.

Instead of

Her hiding place was found by the hunters.

Write:

The hunters found her hiding place.

SLOW PACE

In a slow-paced scene, Passive Voice can sometimes be appropriate – but use it very sparingly, because its effects can make the writing clunky, pompous and dull.

Active Voice is almost always better, even in slow-paced sections.

PROFESSIONAL TIP

Occasionally, Passive Voice can produce a desired special effect. For example, you may want to use it in a slow-paced dialogue section when a pompous bureaucrat speaks. *("Concerns were raised by residents about the condition of the building.")* A couple of Passive Voice sentences will characterise the speaker as stiff and stilted, a stickler for bureaucracy who shies back from action.

But use this trick sparingly.

WHAT NOT TO DO

Don't insert Passive Voice constructions for the sake of slowing pace, or you risk boring the reader.

ASSIGNMENT

Check your fast-paced section: Does it contain any Passive Voice constructions? If yes, change them to Active Voice.

CHAPTER 15

PRESENT PARTICIPLE PHRASES

Present Participle Phrases are actions expressed through the -ing form of the verb. They often stand at the beginning of a sentence.

Snatching her coat, Mary ran to the door.

Clawing with his fingernails, John dug a hole in the ground.

Screaming for help, he hammered at the door.

Listening to Mary's claims, John grew suspicious.

Searching for her wallet, Mary discovered an envelope.

Gasping Mary's name, John sank to the ground.

Laying the book aside, Mary listened to the conversation.

Present Participle Phrases imply that the character is doing two things at once. They can have both a pace-slowing and a pace-increasing effect, so use them with care.

By the way, Present Participle Phrases are a peculiarity of the English language. Other languages either don't have them at all, or with different usages and effects.

FAST PACE

Since this kind of sentence shows the character doing two things at once, they're suitable for fast-paced sections. However, they don't feel super-fast.

Use them when the action is fast – but not for the extremely fast part.

SLOW PACE

In a slow-paced section, Present Participle Phrases serve to 'wake up' the action. Something is happening. The action may be slow, but it's not static.

PROFESSIONAL TIP

Present Participle Phrases are great for the transition from slow- to fast-pace sections.

Here's an example. Mary and John talk about their relationship conflict while eating a picnic lunch – that's slow pace. Then a wildfire approaches and they must run for their lives – that's fast pace.

For the transition from slow to fast, insert a sentence starting with a Present Participle phrase, such as: *Grabbing John by the sleeve, Mary jumped up.*

WHAT NOT TO DO

Don't overuse Present Participle Phrases. Novice writers tend to use them a lot – far too frequently – which leads to a monotonous rhythm. A manuscript full of Present Participle Phrases (especially at the beginning of sentences) signals to the publisher's editor that this is probably a beginner writer – and that's a signal you may not want to send.

ASSIGNMENTS

1. In both the fast- and slow-paced section, find all Present Participle Phrases. Have you overused them (novice flag)? If yes, rewrite some of those sentences.

2. Place one Present Participle Phrase in your writing where it yields the best effect. Choose one of these:

- When the character acts fast, doing two things at the same timeline

- When the action is slow, and you want to 'wake up' the pace a little

- When the action (and the pace) change from slow to fast.

CHAPTER 16

SCENE OPENINGS

At the beginning of each scene, place a hook to draw the reader in. This hook should be something that puts a question in the reader's mind. The ideal question is: "Will the MC achieve this goal?" e.g. "Will he find his sister?" "Can she rescue her friend?" "Will he gain her forgiveness?" Spell the 'scene question' out quite clearly as early as possible in the scene.

Provide at least one important reason why it's so important for the MC to achieve this goal. "He had to find his sister, to redeem himself for his previous failure."

Throughout the scene, remind the reader of this scene question. Perhaps someone mentions it in a conversation, or the MC redoubles his efforts because it's so important to achieve the goal.

FAST PACE

If you write a fast-paced scene without a clear goal and story question, the section can feel rushed and without purpose.

State the goal at the beginning of the scene, together with the reason why it is important. Now the reader is wondering if the MC will achieve it, and root for the MC, racing along through the high-speed action.

To remind the reader of the goal, state it in different ways in very short sentences from the MC's perspective.

Example:

Another corridor. Mary was in one of those rooms. He had to find her.

You can also use dialogue. Keep the sentences very short:

"I must find Mary," he panted. "And I will."

To increase the sense of urgency, introduce a 'ticking clock'. Let the MC race frantically to accomplish his goal before the time runs out:

He checked his watch. Quarter to ten – fifteen minutes before the bomb exploded. He had to find Mary and get her out.

SLOW PACE

At the beginning of a slow-paced scene, state the scene goal and its reasons clearly. You can devote a whole paragraph to it, explaining its importance. You may want to finish the paragraph with a question, spelling out the actual question you want to plant in the reader's mind (e.g. *Could he persuade Mary to forgive him?)*

A slow-paced scene without a story question feels dragging and dull.

Throughout the scene, remind your readers of the story question (whether the MC will achieve his goal, and why it is so important).

WHAT NOT TO DO

Don't write a scene without giving the main character a goal to achieve, or without making that goal clear from the start.

PROFESSIONAL TIP

The following technique is immensely powerful, but it takes advanced writing skills to pull it off.

Use a 'ticking clock' in a slow-paced scene.

This works only in certain situations: Something terrible is about to happen, the MC knows this but can't act to prevent it because he's confined/tied up/imprisoned. In this situation a skilled writer can turn the suspense and tension up so much that the readers will be biting their nails.

I recommend using this only once in a novel, perhaps near the climax.

ASSIGNMENTS

1. Take your fast-paced section – this time the whole scene, even if you've previously worked only on a short excerpt. Is it clear what the MC wants to achieve in this scene, and why? If not, insert a sentence or two at the beginning of the scene to make it clear.

    Find at least one spot in the scene where you can reiterate the scene goal in a terse, breathless way.

2. Take your slow-paced section. Again, this time work with the whole scene. Make sure the reader knows what specific goal the MC is trying to achieve, and find a way to state it clearly at the beginning. You can devote a whole paragraph to it.

    Then find one or more spots in the scene where you can remind the reader of what the MC wants to achieve, and why this is so important.

CHAPTER 17

ENDING A SCENE

The end of a scene is often slower-paced than what came before. This helps the reader to mentally and emotionally process what happened, and leads to a natural break.

The slow section at the end of a scene is often called a 'sequel' – it's where the Point-of-View character analyses what happened and plans what to do next.

However, the pace must not drop to zero, nor must the tension. Place a hook in that section to keep the suspense high.

On finishing the scene, you want your readers to fetch themselves a cup of coffee, pick the kids up from school or get some sleep... and to return to the story as fast as they can. Ideally, the end of each scene should make them keen to read on to find out what will happen next, so they pick up the book again at the earliest opportunity.

At the end of the scene, the reader must clearly know the answer to the scene question posed at the beginning: has the MC achieved his goal? Better than a 'yes' or 'no' answer is a 'yes but' or 'no and furthermore' answer.

Example of a 'yes but' scene ending:

Yes, the university has granted her a sabbatical so she can carry out the archaeological excavation – but the main sponsors have withdrawn their funding.

Example of a 'no and furthermore' scene ending:

No, he has not won his ex-girlfriend's forgiveness – and furthermore, she has become engaged to his best friend.

FAST PACE

If you end a fast-paced scene abruptly, the reader's head is spinning – and not in a good way.

Slow the scene at the end for a 'sequel' to give the character and the reader a chance to catch their breath, process what has happened – and also for the character to decide on the next step.

The 'sequel' section of a fast-paced scene is usually short, sometimes just a paragraph or two, although it can be longer.

How can you segue from fast-paced action to medium- or slow-paced reflection? Here are two ways:

1. If the character has been acting and reacting at high speed in one dangerous situation after another (perhaps fleeing from the crazed axe-murderer), put her in a situation of relative safety. Maybe she's sheltering in a hiding place, hoping that the villain and his henchmen will pass her by. While she's cowering in there, she can't move or do anything. This slows the pace of the action, and allows you to slow the writing. The danger is still there, and the chase can continue in the next scene, but for the moment, the pace slows. The danger might also be over – but the character realises that an even bigger danger lies ahead.

2. If the action is concluded, let the PoV character observe the aftermath. At the end of a battle scene, he may walk across the battlefield, see his slain friends, watch the carrion crows peck at disembowelled bodies, assess the damage inflicted by and on the enemy, feel grief, triumph and other emotions, dress his own and other soldiers' wounds, talk with a brother-in-arms, deal with prisoners of war, speculate on how the overall war is progressing and more.

This not only gives the reader a chance to slow down, but it provides a grounding in the new reality.

This type of 'sequel' can be emotionally harrowing. Its relatively slow pace and emotional intensity create a strong contrast to the previous fast-pace action where the character didn't have time to think or emote.

Either way, embed a hook into this final part – perhaps the character planning the next daring step.

SLOW PACE

If the overall pace of the scene is slow, the ending is probably even slower – but it must not be boring! A good strategy is to focus on emotion. Give the Point-of-View character strong feelings, and let the reader share them.

When the main part of the scene is concluded, the PoV character may spend some time reflecting on what happened, licking her wounds or rejoicing in her triumph. This 'sequel' may take place in a different location. It can be quite long – in some genres the sequel can be as long as the main part of the scene. It may involve another character, e.g. she may discuss the events with her best friend. In this section, the PoV character processes emotionally what happened, and the reader shares this process.

Make sure that the PoV doesn't simply wallow in despair, but forms a resolution. For example, he may grieve that his ex-girlfriend no longer wants him in her life, he may be tormented by anger and jealousy – but then he resolves to prove that he is worthy of her. Or maybe he resolves to join a dating site and find someone new. Whatever suits the plot – comes to a resolution. This resolution is the hook: the reader wants to find out how he's going to prove himself worthy, or how he fares on the dating scene.

PROFESSIONAL TIP

Invest time and creativity in the final paragraph of each scene. Craft it carefully, so it contains a strong hook that drives the reader to the next scene.

WHAT NOT TO DO

Don't end the scene without answering the question you put in the reader's mind at the beginning of the scene.

ASSIGNMENTS

1. Use a fast-paced scene (perhaps the one you've worked with before). Write or rewrite the ending, so that it fulfils these criteria:

    a) it answers the question asked at the beginning (ideally with a 'yes but' or 'no and furthermore' answer)

    b) the pace slows significantly

    c) the main character (and thus the reader) processes what has just happened

    d) a hook motivates the reader to read on

2. Use a slow-paced scene (perhaps the one you've worked with before). Write or rewrite the ending so that it meets these criteria:

    a) it answers the question asked at the beginning (ideally with a 'yes but' or 'no and furthermore' answer)

    b) the pace is slow at the end

    c) the character processes what has just happened in a way that stirs up the reader's emotions

    d) the character resolves to deal with the 'but' or the 'furthermore' and forms at least the rudiments of a plan.

CHAPTER 18

HOW TO VARY THE PACE WITHIN A SCENE

Just as you should vary the pace throughout the story (or novel), it's a good idea to vary the pace within each scene. This prevents monotony and keeps your readers' interest.

Here are guidelines for how you may structure the scene in terms of pacing. These suggestions will not work precisely for every scene, so feel free to adapt them to your scene's content.

STRUCTURE OF A MOSTLY FAST-PACED SCENE

Examples of this type of scene: duellists fighting with swords, the PoV running for her life.

Instead of keeping the pace of the scene relentlessly fast, vary it a little.

1. Start with a few medium-paced paragraphs. (They probably shouldn't be very slow, but slower than what comes next.)

2. Then switch to fast pace. Increase the pace as the action speeds up.

3. If the plot allows, insert a paragraph or several where the pace slows to medium again. This needs to be at a suitable spot, somewhere where the MC takes a break or at least gets a breather. In this section, the PoV character may even think and plan, but not much. The break won't last long.

4. Then speed the pace up again – and if it suits the scene, make it extremely fast, piling on all the fast-pacing techniques you've learnt – short words, very short sentences, sentence fragments – for the climax.

5. End the scene with a medium- or even slow-paced section. The action is over, and the PoV sees the aftermath and resolves what to do next.

STRUCTURE OF A MOSTLY SLOW-PACED SCENE

(Examples for this type of scene: a relationship-conflict between lovers, a police officer interrogating a suspect.)

A whole scene with only slow-paced paragraphs can feel dull, even if the content is rich in emotion and conflict. Vary the pace, switching between slow- and medium-paced paragraphs.

Towards the climax of the scene, when the excitement of the relationship conflict heats up, a medium-paced writing style will emphasise the tension.

For the last few paragraphs, switch to a slower pace again.

PROFESSIONAL TIP

You may want to use highlights in three different colours to categorise each paragraph in the scene according to what kind of pace you want that paragraph to have. (I use yellow for fast, grey for medium, and light blue for slow.) This will give you a good visual overview, and you can adjust the scene's structure if necessary.

Then edit the scene, paragraph by paragraph, until the pace of your writing matches the pace of the content everywhere.

I don't do this with every scene, but find it an eye-opener to do occasionally.

WHAT NOT TO DO:

Don't keep the pace steady for a whole scene. Instead, vary it at least a little, choosing moments when the action speeds up or slows down.

ASSIGNMENTS

Work with whole scenes rather than just scene excerpts for these exercises.

1. Take a fast-paced scene. This can be the scene containing the excerpt you've previously worked with, or a different one.

   Identify the moment(s) when the action is fastest, and apply more fast-pace techniques there.

   At the beginning and the end of the scene, slow the pace. You may decide to add some additional sentences.

   Find a spot in the scene where the fast action slows for a moment. Slow the pacing a little there as well – perhaps simply by removing some surplus fast-pace techniques you've applied.

2. Take the slow-paced scene. Find at least one spot where the action speeds up a little. If there is no action at all, pick the spot where tempers rise and the conflict sharpens. Use some fast-pace techniques there, but apply them in modest doses, so the pace doesn't get really fast.

CHAPTER 19

WHAT TO DO IF THE WHOLE NOVEL FEELS RUSHED

If your critiquers, beta-readers and editors complain that your writing feels superficial and rushed, you have a pacing problem.

Most likely, you have applied fast-pace techniques throughout, and this relentless race leaves the reader out of breath. It also feels monotonous, and it doesn't give your readers the chance to get emotionally involved and savour the story.

Here are four solutions:

1. Identify some sections in your story where the action of the content slows, and focus on slowing the pace to match.

Try to find moments where one of these three situations apply:

- The MC is waiting for someone or something
- The characters are static, maybe sitting around to discuss something
- The MC is confined – maybe imprisoned or injured – and therefore unable to take the required action

In these three types of situations apply slow-pace techniques.

2. Ask your beta-readers (or whoever told you the novel feels rushed) which parts they would like to have slowed down and fleshed out. Consider developing those sections in greater depth.

3. At the end of each scene, insert a brief 'sequel' section in which the main character assesses what has happened, comes to terms with it emotionally, and decides what to do next. Use slow- or medium-pace techniques for this.

4. Insert more descriptions. Describe landscapes, interiors, furnishings, faces, body shapes, objects, sounds, smells. For example, whenever the Point-of-View character enters a new location, add a sentence describing the smells there.

The descriptions don't need to be long: adding a sentence here and there is enough.

ASSIGNMENT

(optional)

If your writing feels rushed, identify several sections in which the content would lend itself to slower-paced writing techniques.

Pick one of those sections, and rewrite it using slow-paced techniques.

CHAPTER 20

WHAT TO DO IF YOUR WHOLE NOVEL DRAGS

Do your beta readers, critiquers, editors tell you that the whole novel is too slow-paced? 'Slow-paced' is often a polite way of saying 'It's boring, it drags.' Critiquers used to say this of my fiction and they were right. Dragging pace was the biggest flaw in my early writing. I've learnt how to fix it, and you can use my techniques.

Fixing a manuscript that drags from beginning to end is the biggest challenge we're tackling in this course. That's why I've left it to near the end. You need to strategically employ several of the fast-pace techniques you've learnt in the preceding chapters, and in addition, you need to address macro issues.

Which of these three root issues are causing the 'slow-paced' (dragging) effect in your book? Be brutally honest with yourself. If necessary, ask writer friends who're not afraid to speak their mind.

Cause 1:

You've used slow-paced writing techniques for the whole story instead of varying the pace.

Solution:

Identify the sections where the action speeds up, and apply fast-paced writing techniques.

Cause 2:

Not enough happens to keep the reader interested. For example, a scene may consist of nothing but two characters having an important conversation over a restaurant meal.

Solutions:

1. Throw additional obstacles at your characters and force them to deal with them – at the same time as they deal with the problems they're already dealing with. What if a fire breaks out in the restaurant while the two characters are having their important conversation? Let them continue talking while they evacuate the building, climbing down the fire escape – the scene will immediately feel faster and more exciting.

2. Layer scenes. Take the events from two or more scenes and condense them into a single one, so that twice as much happens in the short space. The scene where the couple have their important conversation over a restaurant meal could also be the one where his ex-wife bursts in on them to reveal that she's pregnant and the one where his pacemaker fails so he has to be rushed to hospital. Let it all happen at once, and see how the pace accelerates.

Cause 3:

In many sections, nothing happens at all. The character gazes out of the window, or travels through the landscape, observing, thinking, emoting... There's a lot of information and backstory in those pages, but no action.

Solution:

Be ruthless. Cut those sections. Weave small bits of the thoughts and information into other (slow-paced, but not boring) sections.

Please note: some genres naturally call for a slower pace than others. For example, Romance is much slower-paced than Thriller novels. So if a Thriller fan reads a Romance novel for the first time, she may find the pace too slow for her taste. When beta readers comment on pacing, pay attention mostly to people who normally read books in this genre.

ASSIGNMENT

(Optional)

If you're told that your whole writing is 'slow-paced' (or dragging), read one of your works from the perspective of a reader. Identify which of the three causes is at the root of the problem. All three may apply. They did with my early works, which were yawningly dull.

Now try to apply the solution. This may be drastic, it may be painful, and it may need a lot of work. So think about it before you start cutting.

CHAPTER 21

LEARNING FROM OTHER WRITERS

The best way to understand these pacing techniques is to see how they work – or don't work – in other authors' writing.

Learn from both the masters and the pupils. Masters know what they're doing, and by studying their methods, you can enlarge your own toolkit. Novices who haven't mastered pacing yet are even better teachers, because a critical look at their writing can make it immediately clear why something doesn't work.

Try both.

LEARN FROM THE MASTERS

See how the grand masters of fiction use pacing. Next time you read a novel, pay attention to how the pace speeds and slows with the action.

A bestselling thriller published after 1990 is ideal for your analysis. This is because thrillers encompass a wide range of differently-paced scenes from slow to extremely fast, and modern thriller authors are masters at the art of pacing. If the book is a bestseller, it's well written (at least, in the opinion of many readers). I recommend a novel published after 1990s, because not all earlier works are well-crafted in this respect or appeal to modern tastes. In the 19th century, novelists generally wrote in a slow-paced style. As this aspect of fiction gained importance throughout the 20th century, authors learnt from each other and mastered the skill to a higher and higher level.

You may want to use coloured highlighters (if you own the paperback, or if your e-reading app has a highlight function) to mark fast- and slow-paced sections.

Pay attention to the fast-paced sections where the action races and you feel breathless just from reading. What techniques does the author apply?

Then study the slow-paced sections where your breath is normal but your heart clenches. Here, the techniques may be more difficult to identify, but try.

LEARN FROM THE NOVICES

Do you belong to a writers' group or online writing workshop whose members help one another with constructive feedback? Next time you receive a manuscript to critique, observe the pacing. After studying this guide, you can probably spot easily where the writer went wrong – far more easily than in your own writing.

Has the writer rushed a section that needs to be slow, suspenseful and emotionally intense? Or do unnecessary words and excessive descriptions clutter what should be a fast-paced scene, making it a dull, dragging read?

Observing how and why other writers' manuscripts dragged was a huge help to me. After seeing the weakness in other people's writing I could more easily diagnose it in my own. So I recommend that you do this, too.

When phrasing your criticism for novice writers, be tactful. They may not even realise that pacing is an issue, let alone that there are skills and techniques, and may resent getting lectured.

In my experience, it's best to phrase constructive advice for pacing suggestions like this:

"I think this is a very exciting part, but it isn't as good yet as it deserves to be. You could really bring out the excitement of the scene by tightening it. Could you shave off some words?"

"I think this is a really important part of the story, and would like to see it fleshed out more. Perhaps you could add some descriptions of what [X, Y and Z] look like?"

ASSIGNMENTS

1. Study a novel (preferably a recently published bestseller, either a thriller or a novel in your own genre). Pay attention to how the pace slows and speeds up, and how the author adapts the writing style to suit the speed of the action.

   Identify the techniques the author has used. You'll probably recognise some of the techniques we've covered in this guide. Who knows – perhaps you'll even discover another trick you can add to your writing toolkit.

2. Obtain a writer's manuscript draft by volunteering constructive feedback. You can do this by joining a local or online critique workshop or writers' group.

   Your peers (writers at your skill level) will probably be grateful for your help. The works of beginners (less experienced than you) can be an even better source of pacing problems to analyse, but remember that new writers tend to take criticism personally, so be gentle when phrasing your advice.

   The contrast between the masters' and the novices' handling of pace will probably be a real eye-opener for you.

SAMPLE STORY: DOUBLE RAINBOWS

Here's one of my short stories, to show you how I've applied pacing in practice. The story begins with slow pace and ends fast. See if you can identify the techniques I've used, especially at the end where I sped up the pace more and more.

Gerard hurried down the spiral staircase of Sibyl's lighthouse, his shoes clanking on the metal steps. The blue steel hands of his Rolex showed 8.13. The tide had turned two hours ago, and he did not want to get his new boots wet as he hiked home.

The steep chalk path from the promontory to the seabed was slippery with smudge from the night's rain. The sea surface glinted like a diamond-sprinkled sheet, and the air smelled of salty seaweed. In the distance, gulls cackled and squealed.

His chest brimmed with pride at how well he had handled the situation. Breaking to your girlfriend that you would marry someone else required a delicate touch, especially if she was pregnant. At first, she had hurled reprimands. Then she had demanded that he leave her home. But the high tide already submerged the way out, and she had to let him stay the night. After a lot of coaxing and consoling, her rants subsided to sobs. Gently, he pointed out that as an artist, she was above conventions like monogamy and marriage, and that single motherhood was all the rage. When he assured her she would remain the love of his life, and promised to continue his Friday night visits, she had stared at him in wide-eyed wonder. By morning, she had clung to him with surprising passion.

Sibyl had amazing curves, flaming hair and a temper to match, vivid imagination but little practical sense. She refused to sell the dilapidated lighthouse to one of the wealthy buyers queuing for 'converted character properties', insisting she loved living surrounded by sea. Isolated when the tide rose twice a day, with only her paintings for company, she lived for Gerard's weekly visits.

Driftwood, whelk eggs and cuttlefish bones littered the low-tide seabed, and bundles of dark bladderwrack lay entangled like scorched spaghetti. As he skirted around chunky boulders, the smell of fishy seaweed grew stronger, wavering between fresh and foul.

Rust-brown shingle and splinters of flint crunched under his fast steps. He had three miles to cover before the incoming tide wet his feet.

In the east, the sun was already painting the sky a brisk blue, but in the north, a curtain of silver-grey rain still veiled the view. A rainbow beyond the promontory framed the lighthouse in bright glory. He squinted. Was that a second rainbow emerging inside the large one? Even as he looked, the faint hues strengthened. Two rainbows, two women – the perfect omen for his fortunate future. Sibyl had probably spotted it already. He pictured her standing at the large window in her round room, paintbrush in hand, plotting to shape the vision into a painting.

But Gerard had no time to linger and watch the rainbows grow, because the tide waited for no man. Everything about nature – the sun, the rain, the rainbows, the tides – followed complex rhythms, regular but never the same. All was calculable – he patted the tide table in his jeans pocket – yet never quite as expected. Atmospheric pressure, moon phases and such all played a role. Stirred by wind and swelled by the rain, today's sea was already higher than normal.

Waves swished and slurped and rustled across the shingle. He took firm, even steps past black rocks, across broken shells and white crab corpses. Water ran in thin streams between sand and stones, down the almost unnoticeable slope towards the sea.

Soon he would have both: a rich wife and an unconventional mistress. A fair man, he would give both women the attention they deserved, but this required skilful planning. Erica could not be relied upon to show the same flexibility as Sibyl; she might even expect to have her husband to herself. He had to show tact and not spoil her illusions. A job involving absences from home would help, preferably no longer in her father's employ.

At 8.22, he reached the mainland shore where cliffs towered like steep castle walls. Thirteen feet above, sparse grasses grew in cracks, and gorse shrubs clung to precarious holds. Below that, nothing found a grip on the stark rock face, nothing survived the high tide.

He had another hour and a quarter to walk on the seabed to the end of the cliff that lined the shore. The wind rose, whipped up waves and sculpted them into mountain ridges. Puddles filled, and water streamed into rock pools. With the hem of his shirt, he wiped the thin coating of salt from his spectacles, and squinted at the sea. The tide was coming faster than it should.

An illusion, no doubt, from a water level raised by wind and rain. Today's high tide was at 13.01, which meant the sea did not hit the cliff until 10.30, and then he would be past the inaccessible part and on dry secure land.

He checked his watch again, just in case. The blue steel hands on the silvered dial showed 8.28 as it should. A quick glance back revealed the bill already washed by water, the route he had walked submerged by the incoming tide. Only its tip, the rock with the lighthouse, still pointed like an admonishing finger out of the sea. The rainbow was now clearly a double, its colours sharp.

Ignoring natural laws, the water crawled closer, brushing the scattered rocks with angry lashes and frothy caress. Puddles filled and forced Gerard to take big strides from rock to rock.

He checked the tide table, ran his finger down the column for today's high tide. 13.01. He was right, and had an hour and a half to clear the rest of the cliff.

Was the sun supposed to stand so high at half past eight? All he knew was that it rose from the east. On previous walks, he had not paid it much attention. He always left Sibyl's place at low tide, which was a different time every week, so the sun was never in the same place anyway. Though the sun looked high, and the water was close.

What if his watch had stopped? A Swiss Rolex was supposed to be infallible. *Ticke-tac, ticke-tac, ticke-tac,* the watch assured him, and the minute hand moved another notch.

As the water's edge sneaked nearer, he scanned the cliff face for an escape. Surely there was some gap, some path, some stairs hewn into the rock? But he had walked this route on many Saturday mornings, and knew there was none. Thoughts and fears whirled through his mind, questions, worries and doubts.

A drop of sweat slid down his back, and another. Keeping close to the cliff, he marched faster.

Wall-like waves crashed and shoved sheets of white foam at his feet. Tendrils of panic curled into his stomach while gulls glided past in mocking calm.

A cloud blocked out the sun. The air chilled and pimpled the skin on his arms, even as the sweat of fear pasted the shirt to his back. To his left, the cliff stood smooth, steep, merciless.

Salty splashes stained his shoes, sneaked into his socks, soaked his trouser legs. The drum of fear beat in his chest. With the watch pressed to his ear, he ran.

Boom boom boom, his heart thudded. The watch went *ticke-tac, ticke-tac, ticke-tac* above the hiss of the waves.

The water rose fast. Icy wet snaked around his ankles, his calves. Still the cliff stretched without end.

No one could have reset the watch except last night.

Sweet Sybil. So grateful, so forgiving.

The next wave slammed his chest against the rock with ice-cold force.

DEAR READER,

I hope you enjoyed working with this book, and have learnt techniques for honing the pace of your stories. When you compare the 'before' and 'after' versions of the sections you've worked on, you'll probably notice a big difference.

I'd love it if you could post a review on Amazon or some other book site where you have an account and posting privileges. Maybe you can mention what kind of fiction you write, and which of the techniques suit your personal author voice best.

Email me (Rayne) the link to your review, and I'll send you a free review copy (ebook) of one of my other Writer's Craft books. Let me know which one you would like: *Writing Fight Scenes, Writing Scary Scenes, The Word-Loss Diet, Writing About Magic, Writing About Villains, Writing Dark Stories, Euphonics For Writers, Writing Short Stories to Promote Your Novels, Twitter for Writers, Why Does My Book Not Sell? 20 Simple Fixes, Writing Vivid Settings, How To Train Your Cat To Promote Your Book, Writing Deep Point of View, Getting Book Reviews, Novel Revision Prompts, Writing Vivid Dialogue, Writing Vivid Characters, Writing Book Blurbs and Synopses, Writing Vivid Plots, Write Your Way Out Of Depression: Practical Self-Therapy For Creative Writers, Fantasy Writing Prompts, Horror Writing Prompts, How to Write That Scene, More Horror Writing Prompts, Writing Love Scenes, Author Branding, Ghost Writing, Writing Gothic Fiction...* (For a title list with brief descriptions, see this page on my website: https://www.raynehall.com/books-for-writers)

My email is contact@raynehall.com. Drop me a line if you've spotted any typos which have escaped the proofreader's eagle eyes, or want to give me private feedback or have questions.

You can also contact me on Twitter: https://twitter.com/RayneHall. Tweet me that you've read this book and ask me to follow you back, and I probably will.

If you find this book helpful, it would be great if you could spread the word about it. You may know other writers who struggle with pacing issues and would benefit.

At the end of this book, you'll find an excerpt from another Writer's Craft Guide you may find useful, *Writing Vivid Emotions*. Enjoy!

Rayne Hall

ACKNOWLEDGEMENTS

Sincere thanks to the critiquers and beta-readers who helped improve the draft chapters and gave valuable feedback on the completed manuscript: Kim Bonsor, Yolanda McCarthy, Patricia McBride, Susanne McCarthy, Rae Hachton, Sue Johnson Garey Harvey, Alex Harford.

The book cover is by Erica Syverson and Jasmine Bailey. Julia Gibbs proofread the manuscript, and Eled Cernik formatted the book.

I also thank my team of rescue cats – Sulu, Yura, Meli and T'Pau – for being such well-behaved companions who took turns snuggling on the desk between my arms as I was writing. Their purrs are the best inspiration a writer could want.

EXCERPT FROM
WRITING VIVID EMOTIONS:

CHAPTER 2:
VISCERAL RESPONSES

Instead of stating the emotion *(He was angry. She felt desire.)* describe its effects on the body. Every emotion brings physical symptoms. Sometimes we're consciously aware of them, for example, when gross injustice makes us nauseous or the supervisor's constant meddling causes us a painful stiffness at the back of our neck. These physical reactions are so common that they have given rise to the phrases 'this makes me sick' and 'a pain in the neck'.

These visceral reactions serve to convey what the PoV character feels. Where in the body does she feel it? How does it feel? Is the sensation hot or cold, pleasant or painful, expanding or tight? Does it itch, throb, churn or tingle?

Write a sentence about it. You can include the name of the emotion if you wish, although this is often not necessary.

If a fiction character is angry, a novice might write *'he felt angry'* which is bland and leaves the reader untouched.

Now consider an angry person's visceral reactions: churning stomach, acid feeling in the guts, tightness in the diaphragm area, quivering muscles in the upper arms, stiff neck, heat flushing through the body.

You might use these to write one of these sentences:

His stomach churned.

His neck stiffened.

Acid anger rose like undigested food from his stomach.

His biceps quivered, ready for a fight.

Heat washed through him in an angry wave.

He tried to rub the stiffness from his neck.

Let's take another emotion: desire. When a character desires someone or something, the physical symptoms include awareness of one's own heartbeat, warmth flooding the body, increased saliva in the mouth, tingling all over or just in the hands, fingers aching with the need to touch the person or object, faster breath, a pang in the heart area, a pleasant shiver all over or just in the upper body. (Erotic desire brings an additional set of reactions which I won't describe here.)

You might write sentences like these:

Her breath came faster, and her heart danced.

Warmth filled her chest, her heart, her mind.

Her fingers tingled.

Her palms burned with the need to touch his skin.

A pang in her chest released waves of yearning.

To find the right 'symptoms' of an emotion, draw on your own experience. How does desire feel to you? Where in the body have you felt anger?

At the end of this book, I have compiled a thesaurus of visceral reactions where you can look up the emotion and find relevant symptoms.

PROFESSIONAL TIP

To emphasise an emotion, cluster several symptoms. You can sprinkle them across several paragraphs or combine two in a single sentence like this:

Her heart pounded and her mouth went dry. (Fear)

His throat scratched and his vision blurred. (Sadness)

However, it's best not to put more than two visceral responses into one sentence.

WHAT NOT TO DO

Don't apply visceral reactions with a heavy brush. If you overuse them with a symptom in every paragraph of your story, your writing will feel heavy and the readers may find it tedious.

Instead, cluster several visceral responses when you want to emphasise emotions, and keep other sections visceral-free.

ASSIGNMENTS

1. Choose a situation in your work in progress (WiP) where the PoV character experiences an intense emotion: disappointment, jealousy, happiness, whatever.

    Think of a time when you felt disappointed, jealous, happy. Conjure up the memory in detail. After a while, your mind will produce the physical symptoms. Write them down. Then tweak them to suit the character and situation, and insert a sentence or several into the scene.

    You can supplement your memory with suggestions from the Thesaurus of Visceral Reactions Chapter 13.

2. Next time you experience an emotion – frustration, anger, desire, relief, boredom – observe the physical symptoms in

your own body and write them down. You can do this in your journal, or directly into a structured file on your computer you can access easily. If you do this every time, you'll soon have a personal Emotion Descriptions Bank to draw on.

Venting troublesome emotions such as hurt, frustration and resentment on paper can be therapeutic. It's also a constructive use of your time when you're obliged to attend pointless meetings and presentations where the speaker goes on and on. Take your notebook and describe your symptoms of boredom – drowsiness, wandering attention, the need to clench your jaw to prevent a yawn. If you do this, others will think you're an attentive, note-taking listener, never guessing that you are working on a creative writing project.

Made in the USA
San Bernardino, CA
22 December 2019